CRDE

SMNES

Max Wainewright

First published in Great Britain in 2020
by Wayland

Editor: Elise Short
Designer: Matt Lilly
Cover Design: Peter Scoulding
Illustrations: John Haslam

HB ISBN: 978 1 5263 1331 7
PB ISBN: 978 1 5263 1332 4

Printed and bound in Dubai

MIX
Paper from
responsible sources
FSC® C104740

Picture credits:
Adventtr/iStock: 5. GodfriedEdelman/iStock:
7t. Lluis Gene/AFP/Getty Images: 4bl. Rui
Matos/Dreamstime: 5tl. Robert_s and NASA/
Shutterstock: 20b, 21tl, 21c.

Every attempt has been made
to clear copyright. Should there be any
inadvertent omission please apply to the
publisher for rectification.

Wayland
An imprint of
Hachette Children's Group
Part of Hodder and Stoughton
Carmelite House
50 Victoria Embankment
London EC4Y 0DZ

An Hachette UK Company
www.hachette.co.uk
www.hachettechildrens.co.uk

We recommend that children are supervised at all times when using the Internet. Some of the projects in this series use a computer webcam or microphone. Please make sure children are made aware that they should only allow a computer to access the webcam or microphone on specific websites that a trusted adult has told them to use. We do not recommend children use websites or microphones on any websites other than those mentioned in this book.

Contents

For help with any of the projects go to: www.maxw.com

Smartphones

Smartphones have become a big part of our lives. People use them to find out the weather, send messages, listen to music, check their email, play games and even make telephone calls!

Mobile phones came before smartphones. Early ones were not that mobile!

The first wireless telephones were developed over a hundred years ago, but were not very portable. Technology evolved and by the 1950s it was possible to have a phone in a car, but it could only be used to make phone calls.

In 1983 phones that could actually be carried around were introduced, but were very expensive and heavy. As mobile phones continued to develop, more features were added. What is considered to be the world's first smartphone wasn't introduced until 1993. It did more than just make phone calls, allowing people to send and receive fax messages and emails, as well as having applications, such as a calendar and calculator.

The IBM Simon was probably the first ever smartphone.

By the early 2000s phones with access to emails and the Internet became more common. These smartphones still had keyboards.

A big change came at the end of 2006 when the Korean company LG made a phone with a large touchscreen replacing the keyboard.

That looks more like my phone!

Inside A Smartphone

Let's have a look inside a modern smartphone - but don't try taking yours apart!

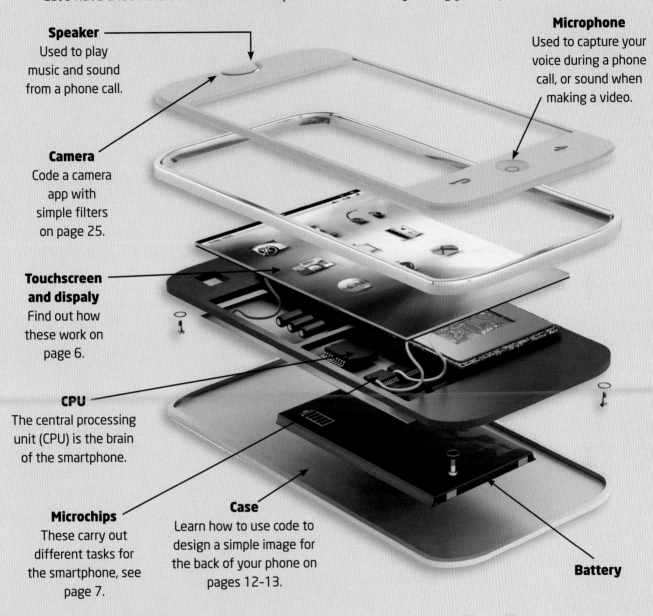

Speaker
Used to play music and sound from a phone call.

Microphone
Used to capture your voice during a phone call, or sound when making a video.

Camera
Code a camera app with simple filters on page 25.

Touchscreen and dispaly
Find out how these work on page 6.

CPU
The central processing unit (CPU) is the brain of the smartphone.

Microchips
These carry out different tasks for the smartphone, see page 7.

Case
Learn how to use code to design a simple image for the back of your phone on pages 12-13.

Battery

APPS AND CODING

Programs that run on a smartphone are known as apps. All programs are built using code. There are many different ways to create programs and apps. In this book we will look at some simple methods using Scratch. If you want to find out more about Scratch see page 30.

A 'proper' app has its own icon on the homescreen of a phone. To build apps like this you need to use special software. We will be using one called App Inventor for most of the projects in this book. Go to pages 14-17 to learn how to access App Inventor.

Inside a Smartphone

Touch Screens

There are different methods to make touch screens work. Most smartphones use capacitive technology that works out exactly where the screen has been touched. Some use a sensor in each corner of the screen, others use a grid of wires directly behind the glass of the screen.

Thousands of incredibly thin wires are connected horizontally and vertically across the screen to form a grid. When someone touches the screen the amount of electricity or voltage in the wires drops. A microprocessor notices where the voltage dropped and which wires were near that point. This allows it to work out the exact position of the touch.

Screens and Co-ordinates

Smartphone screens are made up of hundreds of thousands of tiny squares called pixels. These pixels are laid out in a grid, so each pixel has an x and y co-ordinate. Software in the smartphone enables coders to work with the pixels either by instructing a particular pixel to show a specific colour, or working out which pixel is nearest to where a user touched the screen.

> **The width and height of a smartphone screen is called its resolution. Modern phones have a resolution of 1920 x 1080 pixels or more.**

How big is your computer browser in pixels?

> **On a desktop or laptop computer you can find out how big the web browser you are using is by typing some code.**

1. To display the developer console, start up your web browser. If you are using Chrome, click **View > Developer > Developer Tools**.

2. The developer console will be shown here. Click inside it.

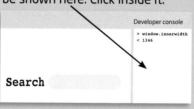

3. Type **window.innerWidth** and press enter.

4. Next type **window.innerHeight** and press enter.

```
Developer console
> window.innerwidth
< 1346
> window.innerheight
< 927
```

> **The width and height of the screen in pixels will be displayed.**

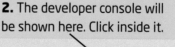

Microchips

Many of the elements that make a smartphone are built from different specialised microchips. They are tiny electrical components that contain millions of minute electrical transistors that carry out special tasks. They are combined with sensors and other components to handle the tasks presented below.

Accelerometer

The accelerometer chip can tell what angle the smartphone is being held at or if it is being shaken. This can be used as a way of controlling games or to make sure the screen is still readable if the screen is upside down.

GPS Chips

These can tell exactly where the smartphone is by communicating with satellites. Find out more and build a simple map app on pages 20-21.

Memory Chips

Memory chips are used to store things that are created by the person using the phone. These include photos, videos, notes and pretty much everything that you add to your phone including apps.

Everything on your phone is stored as millions of zeroes and ones, called binary code.

Storing Sounds

Sound is turned into digital information or data so it can be stored on your phone. This enables it to be recorded or played back.

Streaming Music

Storing music takes up quite a lot of space. Streaming music apps allow you to play songs that aren't actually stored on your phone. The music is downloaded a few seconds at a time from a music website.

Texting

You're probably quite used to sending text messages. Can your remember the first one you sent?

The very first text message was sent on 3 December 1992. An engineer called Neil Papworth typed 'Merry Christmas' on his computer and sent it to a colleague's mobile phone.

Across the entire world, around 16 million texts are sent every minute.

How does text messaging work?

To: Sam

Meet you at 6.

Send

+44 7929 11..

53 65 65 20
79 6F 75 20
61 74 20
36

1. You type a message on your smartphone and tap send.

2. The letters in your message are converted into a special code called GSM7.

Sending...

3. Your phone transmits the code as a radio signal.

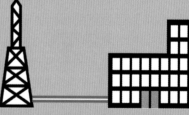

4. The nearest phone mast receives a radio signal containing your message.

5. The phone mast sends the message to a central exchange or control centre.

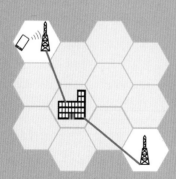

6. Now the central exchange has to work out where the message needs to be sent. Earth is divided up into different sections or 'cells', each with its own phone mast. Smartphones regularly update their network to tell them which cell they are in. The central exchange then sends the message to the mast in the cell the receiver's phone is in.

Meet you at 6.

7. The phone mast then sends the message to the receiving phone. It is converted from GSM7 code and finally shown on the screen as a new message.

Code Your Own Emojis

One of the fun things about texting is sending emojis. Let's code our own.

STEP 1: Start Scratch

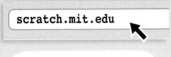

Open your web browser and type in **scratch.mit.edu**

Press the **enter** key.

Click **create** to get started.

We're going to draw lots of circles to make the emojis, so let's set up our own code block to do this.

The block will determine where each circle is drawn. We can use x and y values for this. It will also set its size (diameter).

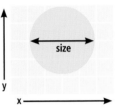

STEP 2: Make a block

Click on **My Blocks**.

Click on **Make a Block**.

Type **circle**.

Add an input number or text

We need to give the circle block *three* values (x, y and size), so click **Add an input** *three* times.

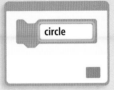

Type in the names of three inputs **x**, **y** and **size**.

OK Click **OK**.

STEP 3: The pen

We need to add extra code blocks that let us draw while the code is running. This group of code blocks is called an extension.

Click the **Add Extension** icon.

Click on **Pen**.

STEP 4: Code it!

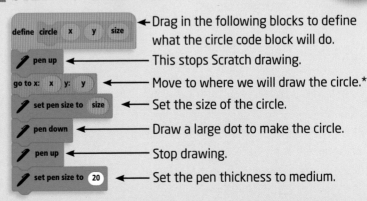

define circle x y size → Drag in the following blocks to define what the circle code block will do.

pen up ← This stops Scratch drawing.

go to x: x y: y ← Move to where we will draw the circle.*

set pen size to size ← Set the size of the circle.

pen down ← Draw a large dot to make the circle.

pen up ← Stop drawing.

set pen size to 20 ← Set the pen thickness to medium.

*Drag the pink x and y blocks from the 'define circle' block above.

STEP 5: Happy coding!

Now drag in this code to draw a happy emoji:

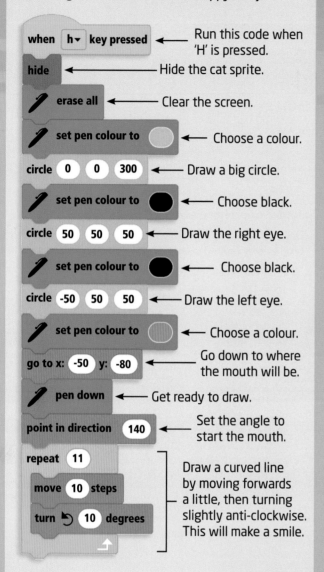

when h ▾ key pressed ← Run this code when 'H' is pressed.

hide ← Hide the cat sprite.

erase all ← Clear the screen.

set pen colour to ← Choose a colour.

circle 0 0 300 ← Draw a big circle.

set pen colour to ⬤ ← Choose black.

circle 50 50 50 ← Draw the right eye.

set pen colour to ⬤ ← Choose black.

circle -50 50 50 ← Draw the left eye.

set pen colour to ← Choose a colour.

go to x: -50 y: -80 ← Go down to where the mouth will be.

pen down ← Get ready to draw.

point in direction 140 ← Set the angle to start the mouth.

repeat 11

　move 10 steps

　turn ↺ 10 degrees

Draw a curved line by moving forwards a little, then turning slightly anti-clockwise. This will make a smile.

STEP 7: Unhappy

Edit the duplicated code so it looks like this:

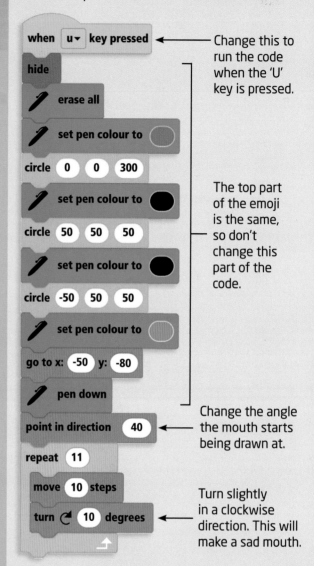

when u ▾ key pressed ← Change this to run the code when the 'U' key is pressed.

hide

erase all

set pen colour to

circle 0 0 300

set pen colour to ⬤

circle 50 50 50

set pen colour to ⬤

circle -50 50 50

set pen colour to

go to x: -50 y: -80

pen down

The top part of the emoji is the same, so don't change this part of the code.

point in direction 40 ← Change the angle the mouth starts being drawn at.

repeat 11

　move 10 steps

　turn ↻ 10 degrees ← Turn slightly in a clockwise direction. This will make a sad mouth.

Press 'H' on your keyboard to test the code and draw a happy emoji!

Press 'U' to draw an unhappy emoji.

STEP 6: Duplicate

Now to make an unhappy emoji. Most of the code will be the same - we just need to turn the mouth upside-down. To save time, let's duplicate the happy code then change a few blocks.

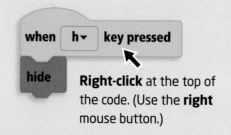

when h ▾ key pressed

hide

Right-click at the top of the code. (Use the **right** mouse button.)

Duplicate

Click **duplicate**.

3 END

648.5 /HOM

219010355
646.436 /ART

219010356
649.125 /HEA

219010357
796.358 /SPO

219010358
636.0887 /HOM

219010359
649.122 /HEA

219010360
200 /COU

ACCN NUMBERS 2190(

STEP 8: Angry!

Now code an angry emoji. You might decide to duplicate some blocks from the other emojis.

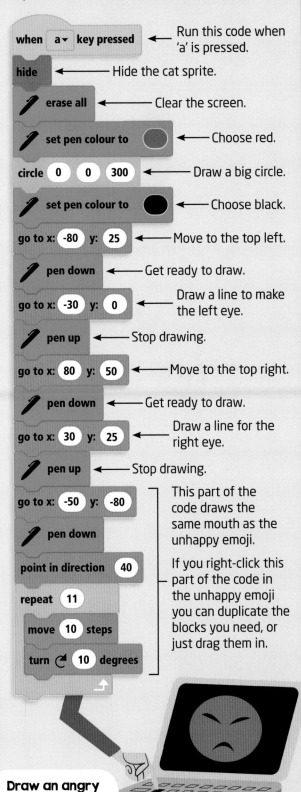

when a ▾ key pressed ← Run this code when 'a' is pressed.

hide ← Hide the cat sprite.

🖊 erase all ← Clear the screen.

🖊 set pen colour to ⬤ ← Choose red.

circle 0 0 300 ← Draw a big circle.

🖊 set pen colour to ⬤ ← Choose black.

go to x: -80 y: 25 ← Move to the top left.

🖊 pen down ← Get ready to draw.

go to x: -30 y: 0 ← Draw a line to make the left eye.

🖊 pen up ← Stop drawing.

go to x: 80 y: 50 ← Move to the top right.

🖊 pen down ← Get ready to draw.

go to x: 30 y: 25 ← Draw a line for the right eye.

🖊 pen up ← Stop drawing.

go to x: -50 y: -80

🖊 pen down

point in direction 40

repeat 11

move 10 steps

turn ↻ 10 degrees

This part of the code draws the same mouth as the unhappy emoji.

If you right-click this part of the code in the unhappy emoji you can duplicate the blocks you need, or just drag them in.

Draw an angry emoji by pressing the 'a' key.

The History of Emojis

Emojis are special graphics or icons that have been designed to show information instead of using words. The first emojis were created in Japan in around 1998. Before that people sometimes combined letters and symbols together to create 'emoticons', such as :-) to show a happy face - but you had to put your head on one side to read them!

■ EXPERIMENT

What other emojis can you draw? Here are some ideas to get you started.

Surprised

Use the code to draw the eyes from the happy emoji. Draw a smaller circle to make the mouth.

Crying

Start with the unhappy emoji and duplicate it. Add two or more light blue circles to make tears.

Winking

Duplicate the happy emoji code and remove one of the eyes. Adapt the line drawing method from the angry eyes to make a straight line.

Experiment and create more emojis of your own!

Phone Case Design

Let's create a phone case design using Scratch.

STEP 1: Start Scratch

 scratch.mit.edu

Open your web browser and type in **scratch.mit.edu**

Press the **enter** key.

Click **create** to get started.

STEP 2: No cats

Sprite1

Click the blue x to delete the cat sprite.

STEP 3: New sprite

Click the **Choose a Sprite** button.

STEP 4: Choose your pattern

Taco

Scroll through the sprites until you find one you want to use.

Click on it to select the image for your phone case pattern.

STEP 5: Code the pattern

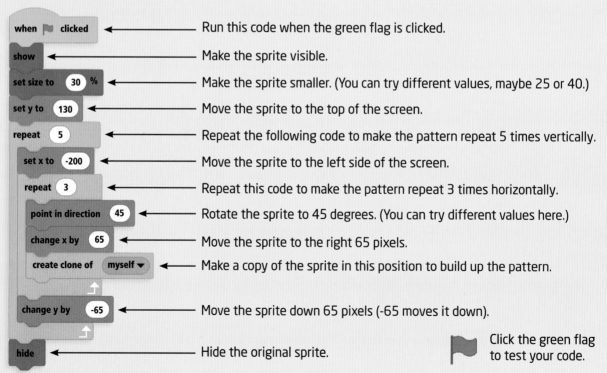

when ▶ clicked — Run this code when the green flag is clicked.

show — Make the sprite visible.

set size to 30 % — Make the sprite smaller. (You can try different values, maybe 25 or 40.)

set y to 130 — Move the sprite to the top of the screen.

repeat 5 — Repeat the following code to make the pattern repeat 5 times vertically.

set x to -200 — Move the sprite to the left side of the screen.

repeat 3 — Repeat this code to make the pattern repeat 3 times horizontally.

point in direction 45 — Rotate the sprite to 45 degrees. (You can try different values here.)

change x by 65 — Move the sprite to the right 65 pixels.

create clone of myself ▼ — Make a copy of the sprite in this position to build up the pattern.

change y by -65 — Move the sprite down 65 pixels (-65 moves it down).

hide — Hide the original sprite.

Click the green flag to test your code.

STEP 6: Draw the case

First add the **Pen extension** as on page 9, step 3.
Then, drag in this code so it follows on from the hide block:

hide

set y to 135 — Move the sprite near the top of the screen.

set pen size to 65 — Ready to draw a very thick line.

erase all — Clear anything drawn previously.

set pen colour to ○ — Set the colour for the case's background.

pen down — Start drawing.

repeat 54 — Repeat the following code 54 times:

change y by -5 — Move the sprite a little way down the screen.

set x to -140 — Move the sprite to the left.

change x by 140 — Move it to the right to draw horizontally.

pen up — Stop drawing.

STEP 7: Download and print

Click the **Full Screen** button to enlarge the pattern (top right corner of the screen).

Right-click the case, then click **Save Image As**.

case.png Save

Save it, then open the file.

Print out your case.

The size it prints at will depend on your computer. You should be able to adjust this on the print dialog box.

STEP 8: Draw round it

Put your phone on top of the print out and carefully draw round it.

STEP 9: Cut it out

Carefully cut it out.

Now you can put your design inside a clear phone case!

Building Apps

**Now its time to build some simple apps!
Let's start by setting up your computer.**

Ask permission from an adult before entering the information to create an account.

STEP 1: Create a Google account

To be able to log in to App Inventor and save apps you need a Google account. Ask an adult if you can create one or if they have one you can use.

Search for **create Google account**.

| create Google account | **Search** ◄

https://accounts.google.com/signup?hl=en

Create your Google Account

STEP 2: Log in

Log into your Google account.

STEP 3: Visit the App Inventor website

Type in **appinventor.mit.edu**.

appinventor.mit.edu

Click **Create Apps**.

Create apps! ◄

If you have an Android device, follow the next steps:

STEP 1: Download the Companion app

This will let you test your apps on your Android device.

Search for **App Inventor companion app**.

| App Inventor companion app |

Search ◄

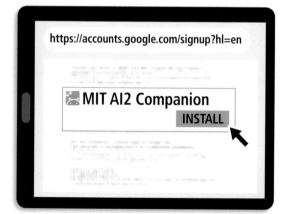

https://accounts.google.com/signup?hl=en

MIT AI2 Companion
INSTALL

Tap **INSTALL** and follow the instructions.

STEP 2: Connect App Inventor to the app

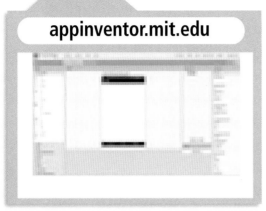

appinventor.mit.edu

Go back to your computer and make sure you are on the App Inventor site. Click **Create apps**.

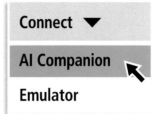

Connect ▼

AI Companion

Emulator

Click the Connect menu, then choose **AI Companion**.

A QR code like this will appear on your computer.

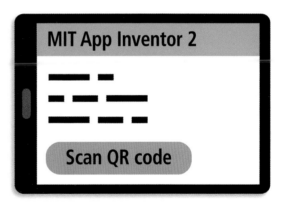

MIT App Inventor 2

Scan QR code

Tap the **Scan QR code** button and hold your device camera up to the QR code on the computer screen.

App Inventor should now be connected to your Android device.

If App Inventor doesn't connect to your device, try closing your web browser. On your device, tap the recent apps button then find the MIT AI2 Companion App icon and close it. Restart the Companion app and then restart the web browser on your computer. Follow the instructions in step 2 to reconnect. If you still have problems connecting, go to the App Inventor site, click **Resources** then **Troubleshooting**.

STEP 1: Download the emulator

Ask an adult before you start installing a program. This program lets you test your apps on your computer screen using a 'virtual Android device'.

Search for **download app inventor emulator**.

download app inventor emulator

Search

http://appinventor.mit.edu/explore/ai2/setup-emulator.html

Choose Mac or PC then follow the instructions to download the emulator.

STEP 2: Install the emulator

Some web browsers will then ask you to run the installation program. Choose **Run**.

If this does not happen, don't panic. The installer file should have downloaded to your computer. Look for it in your downloads folder. Double-click it to start installing the emulator. You should get a big grey box giving you instructions on what to do next. Follow these instructions to complete the installation.

Installing...

If you are on a Mac, you may get a security message. To install the app you will need to click **System Preferences**, click **Security** and change your settings to allow apps to run from **Anywhere**. Search for **install from unknown developer Mac**, for more help.

STEP 3: Install the emulator

If you are using a Mac you can skip this part.

On a PC, App Inventor needs a special program to help it start up the emulator. This is called the AI starter. After you have installed the emulator it should run the AI starter. The next time you use it you will need to start it from the Windows Start menu. It will be in the MIT App Inventor group or in the Recently Added section.

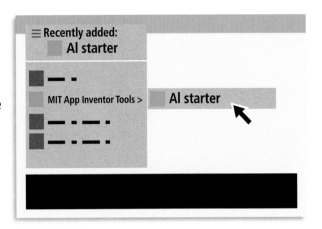

STEP 4: Connect App Inventor to the emulator:

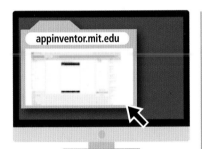

Go back to the App Inventor website. Arrange your screen so the web browser only fills part of the screen. Click **Create apps**.

Click the **Connect** menu, then choose **Emulator**.

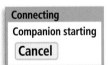

You should see a message telling you to wait whilst the emulator starts. Be patient - this may take a minute or two.

When the emulator has finished setting up, the app you are starting to build will be shown on your computer screen.

App Inventor should now be connected to your emulator.

If App Inventor doesn't connect up to your emulator, try closing the emulator, closing the web browser and starting over again from step 3. If you still have problems connecting go to the App Inventor site, click **Resources** then **Troubleshooting**.

Web Browser

Let's build a basic web browser to visit your favourite websites.

STEP 1: Start App Inventor

Open your web browser and visit **appinventor.mit.edu**.

Click **Create apps**.

STEP 2: Log in

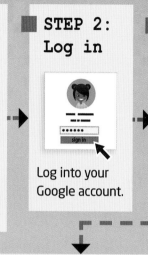

Log into your Google account.

STEP 3: Start a new project

At the top left of the screen click the **Start new project** button.

Type **web** as a file name and click **OK**.

STEP 4: Start designing

We need to add several buttons to the app. A layout component keeps them lined up together. Click the **Layout** group, then drag the **HorizontalArrangement** component on to the viewer.

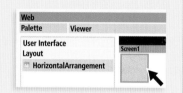

STEP 5: Add three buttons

Next click the **User Interface** group and drag a **Button** into the **HorizontalArrangement** component.

Drag two more buttons on top of the first one so you have three buttons as above.

STEP 6: Set button text

Find the **Properties** box on the right side.

Find the **Text** property. Change the text of the first button to **YouTube**.

Click the second button and change it to say **Google**. Change the third button to say **MaxW**.

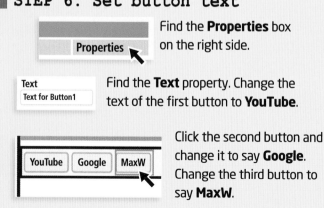

STEP 7: The web component

Drag a **WebViewer** component on to the viewer, beneath the buttons.

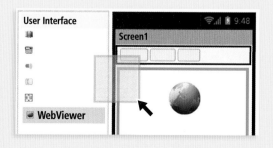

Finding blocks

The pink, orange and blue blocks can be found by looking for the block group with the correct colour.

The brown, dark green and purple blocks are different. To find them, see which component they add code for.

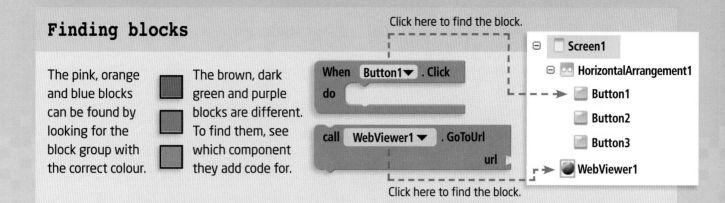

Click here to find the block.

When **Button1 ▼** . Click
do

call **WebViewer1 ▼** . GoToUrl
url

Click here to find the block.

⊟ ☐ **Screen1**
　⊟ ▦ **HorizontalArrangement1**
　　→ ▦ **Button1**
　　　▦ **Button2**
　　　▦ **Button3**
　→ ⬤ **WebViewer1**

STEP 8: Add code

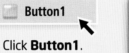

Click the **Blocks** button in the top right corner of the screen.

Button1

Click **Button1**.

When **Button1 ▼** . Click
Do

Drag a **when Button1. Click** block into the code viewer.

Click the **WebViewer1** component, then drag the purple blocks into your code. You will find the pink blocks in the **Text** group.

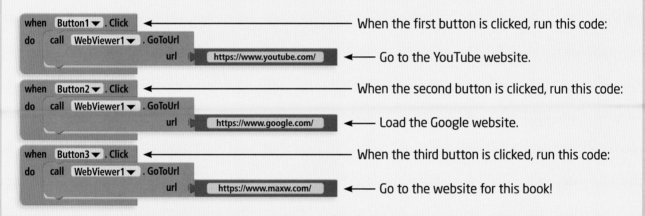

when **Button1 ▼** . Click
do　call **WebViewer1 ▼** . GoToUrl
　　　　url　`https://www.youtube.com/`

When the first button is clicked, run this code:
Go to the YouTube website.

when **Button2 ▼** . Click
do　call **WebViewer1 ▼** . GoToUrl
　　　　url　`https://www.google.com/`

When the second button is clicked, run this code:
Load the Google website.

when **Button3 ▼** . Click
do　call **WebViewer1 ▼** . GoToUrl
　　　　url　`https://www.maxw.com/`

When the third button is clicked, run this code:
Go to the website for this book!

STEP 9: Test the app

Connect ▼
AI Companion
Emulator

Click the **Connect** menu, then choose the **AI Companion** if you are using an Android Device or **Emulator** if you have installed it instead (see pages 16-17 for help).

If you are using the emulator on a PC make sure you have AI starter running. On a Mac, it should start by itself.

If you are using an Android device, start the MIT AI Companion app, then connect it to your computer with the QR code option (see pages 14-15 for more help).

■ EXPERIMENT

Add another website button to your app. Add text to the button (see step 6), then add code to the new button (see step 9) to make it show the new site when it is clicked.

Your web browser app should start running. Try tapping one of the buttons to change the page.

Location Services

One of the most useful apps on a smartphone is the map. As well as carrying a map of the entire world in your pocket, a smartphone map can tell you exactly where you are. But how does that work? Let's find out.

Part 1: How far away is a satellite?

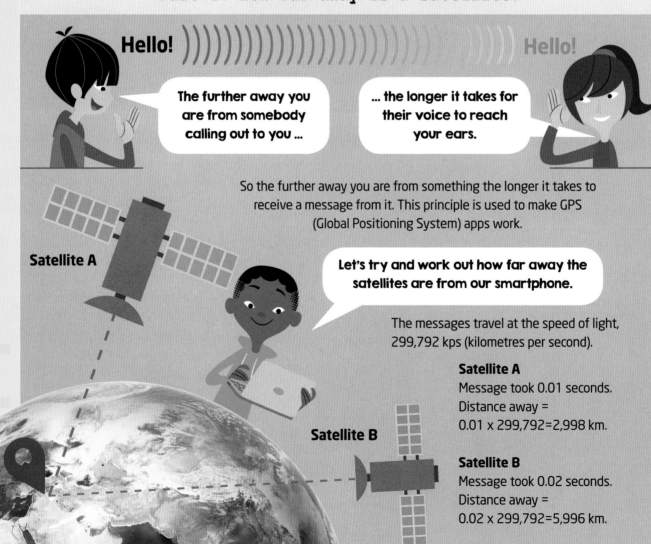

Hello!))))))))))))))))))))))))) Hello!

The further away you are from somebody calling out to you ...

... the longer it takes for their voice to reach your ears.

So the further away you are from something the longer it takes to receive a message from it. This principle is used to make GPS (Global Positioning System) apps work.

Satellite A

Let's try and work out how far away the satellites are from our smartphone.

The messages travel at the speed of light, 299,792 kps (kilometres per second).

Satellite A
Message took 0.01 seconds.
Distance away =
0.01 x 299,792=2,998 km.

Satellite B

Satellite B
Message took 0.02 seconds.
Distance away =
0.02 x 299,792=5,996 km.

Part 2: Intersecting lines

We know that the smartphone must be 2,998 km from satellite A. So it will be somewhere on the dotted red line.

It also must be 5,996 km from satellite B - somewhere on the dotted green line.

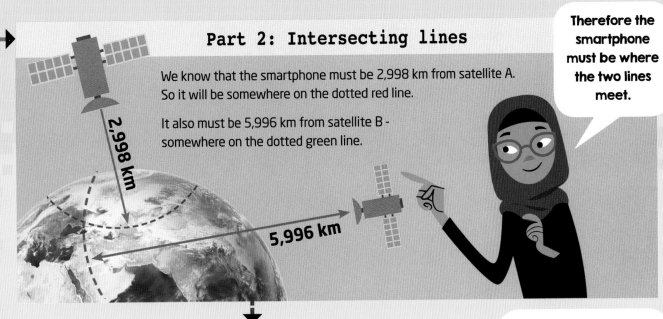

2,998 Km

5,996 km

Therefore the smartphone must be where the two lines meet.

Part 3: Calculating your position

Altogether there are over 30 satellites orbiting Earth, transmitting messages. Each message contains the location of the satellite and what time the message was sent.

We only need two satellites to get a good idea of where the smartphone might be. By using a third satellite the smartphone GPS software makes sure that there is only one possible location for the smartphone. A fourth satellite is used for accuracy: it checks when the time signals were sent.

PRIVACY

It can be useful for trusted members of your family to know where you are. But you don't want everyone else to know. So learn how to use the location services options in your privacy settings.

LONGITUDE AND LATITUDE

There is a co-ordinate system to locate any place on planet Earth called longitude and latitude. Latitude tells us how far north or south a point is from the equator. Longitude measures how far east or west a place is from the Greenwich meridian in London, UK.

To find the longitude and latitude of the town where you live:

1. Go to Google and search for your town.
2. Click on 'maps'. A map of your town should appear.
3. Right-click your mouse on part of the map.
4. Click 'What's here?'
5. A box will appear at the bottom of the page showing the longitude and latitude of the town.

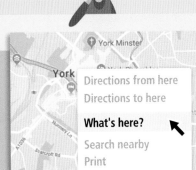

Directions from here
Directions to here
What's here?
Search nearby
Print

City Centre
York
53.960496 – 1.084670

Map App

Now let's build a simple map app that shows the UK,
where your local town and school is.

STEP 1: Start App Inventor

Open your web browser and visit **appinventor.mit.edu**.

Click **Create apps**.

STEP 2: Log in

Log into your Google account.

STEP 3: Start a new project

At the top left of the screen click the **Start new project** button.

Type **maps** as a file name and click **OK**.

STEP 4: Start designing

Click the **Maps** group. Drag a **Map** component on to the viewer.

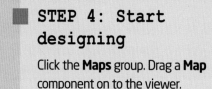

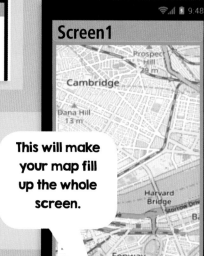

STEP 5: Set the map size

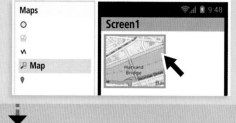

Find the **Height** property. Set it to **Fill parent** then click **OK**.

Find the **Width** property. Set it to **Fill parent** then click **OK**.

This will make your map fill up the whole screen.

STEP 6: Make a box for buttons

We will need to add three buttons to the app. A layout component keeps them lined up together. Click the **Layout** group, then drag the **HorizontalArrangement** component below the map.

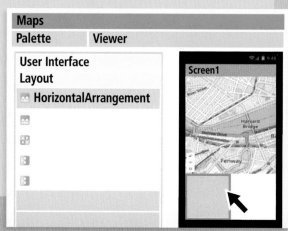

STEP 7: Add three Buttons

Next click the **User Interface** group, then drag a **Button** into the **HorizontalArrangement** component.

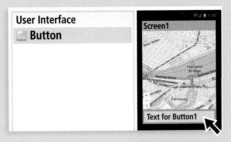

Drag two more buttons on top of the first one so you have three buttons as above.

STEP 8: Set button text

Select the first button.

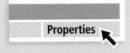

Find the **Properties** box on the right-hand side.

Find the **Text** property. Change the text of the first button to **UK**.

Click the second button and change it to say **Town**. Change the third button to say **School**.

STEP 9: Add code

Click the **Blocks** button in the top right corner of the screen.

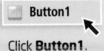

Click **Button1**.

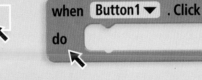

Drag a **when Button1. Click** block into the code viewer.

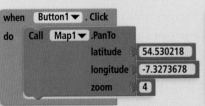

```
when  Button1 ▼ . Click
do   Call  Map1 ▼ .PanTo
              latitude    54.530218
              longitude   -7.3273678
              zoom        4
```

This code will set the map position to show the UK when you click it.

```
when  Button2 ▼ . Click
do   Call  Map1 ▼ .PanTo
              latitude    51.59
              longitude   -0.14753
              zoom        15
```

```
when  Button3 ▼ . Click
do   Call  Map1 ▼ .PanTo
              latitude    51.55814
              longitude   -0.17654
              zoom        15
```

These two blocks of code will make the map focus on your local town or school. Use the instructions on page 21 to work out the latitude and longitude values. Experiment with the zoom value to make it bigger or smaller.

STEP 10: Test the App

Click the **Connect** menu, then choose the **AI Companion** if you are using an Android device or **Emulator** (see pages 16–17 for help).

If you are using the emulator on a PC make sure you have AI starter running.

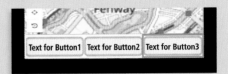

If you are using an Android device start the MIT AI Companion App and connect it with the QR code option (see pages 14–15 for help).

Your App should start up. Click the buttons to make the map show each of the locations.

Camera Technology

One of the most entertaining features of a smartphone is the camera.

In the 19th century, taking a picture was fiddly and required the subject to stay still for a long time.

The first cameras were developed around 200 years ago. They were quite large and heavy to carry around. Cameras stored pictures on film. This made them expensive to use – and you never really knew if your picture was a good one until it was 'developed' (printed out) by a special camera shop. Now you can carry a camera in your pocket.

But how does it work?

When a photo is taken, light reflecting off the subject passes through the lens of the smartphone. It goes through a special filter which breaks down the light into its red, green and blue components. Red, green and blue light then shines onto a special CMOS sensor, which detects how bright the light is.

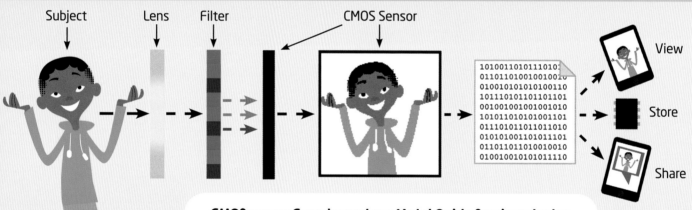

Subject Lens Filter CMOS Sensor View Store Share

```
1010011010111010
1101101001001001
0100101010100110
1011101011011011
0010010010010010
1010110101001101
0111010110110110
0101010011010111
0110110110100100
0100100101011110
```

The CMOS sensor looks at the image one row at a time. It converts each pixel into a number, depending on how much red, green and blue light it can detect. The number is then turned into binary code – a long number made up of ones and zeroes.

CMOS means Complementary Metal Oxide Semiconductor. It is a special sensing and processing microchip.

The picture can then be viewed on the screen of the camera, stored in its memory chips and shared with your friends!

Have fun with your smartphone camera, but think before sharing photos. Don't share any photos you wouldn't want another family member or even a complete stranger to see.

Photo Filter App

Now let's build a simple photo filter app. You'll be able to take a photo, then add funny ears and a nose. You'll learn how to add code that lets you drag the ears and nose around the screen. Finally you'll learn how to save the new image.

STEP 1: Start App Inventor

Open your web browser and visit **appinventor.mit.edu**.

appinventor.mit.edu

Click **Create apps**.

Create apps!

STEP 2: Log in

Log into your Google account.

sign in

STEP 3: Start a new project

Start new project

At the top left of the screen click the **Start new project** button.

Create new App Inventor project

Project name: **Filter**

Cancel   OK

Type **Filter** as a file name and click **OK**.

STEP 4: Add a camera component

The **Camera** component is the most important part of this app.

Media

Choose the **Media** group from the Palette.

Find the Camera component.

Drag it on to the middle of the screen.

It will be shown below the device.

STEP 5: Prepare the layout

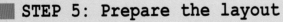

We will need two buttons in the app. Click the **Layout** group, then drag the **HorizontalArrangement** component on to the viewer. This will keep our buttons aligned.

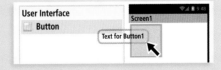

Next click the **User Interface** group, then drag a **Button** into the **HorizontalArrangement** component.

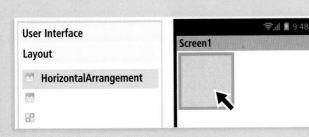

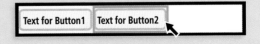

Drag another button on top of the first one so you have two buttons.

STEP 6: Set button text

Select the first button.

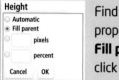

Find the **Properties** box on the right hand side.

Find the **Text** property. Change the text of the first button to **Snap**.

Click the second button and change it to **Save**.

STEP 7: Add the canvas

Drawing and Animation

Choose the **Drawing and Animation** group from the Palette.

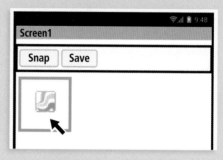

Drag a **Canvas** component on to the screen below the buttons.

Now we need to find some transparent images to use for our filter.

STEP 8: Set canvas size

Find the **Height** property. Set it to **Fill parent** then click **OK**.

Find the **Width** property. Set it to **Fill parent** then click **OK**.

Transparent images have no background, so they look good on top of a photo.

Not transparent

Transparent

STEP 9: Add three sprites

Drag an **ImageSprite** on top of the canvas component.

Drag two more **ImageSprites** on top of the canvas component.

The ImageSprites will be used to store the small filter graphics (like rabbit ears). The canvas keeps them together and stores the photo we will take.

STEP 10: Download images

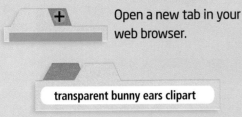

Open a new tab in your web browser.

transparent bunny ears clipart

Search for **transparent bunny ears clipart**.

Images

Click **Images**.

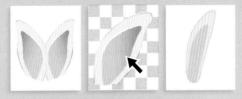

Click one (transparent images are often shown with a grey checked background). Download a few extra so you can experiment.

Right-click the image and click **Save Image As**.

STEP 11: Upload images

Now upload your first image to App Inventor:

Media

Upload File ...

Click **Upload File**. (bottom right of the screen).

Upload file ...

Choose File ...

Cancel   OK

Click **Choose File ...** Browse for the image you downloaded. Then click **OK**.

Media

earL.png

Upload file ...

Your image should now be listed in the Media window.

Media

earL.png

earR.png

nose.png

Upload file ...

Click **Upload** again and add the other images for your filter.

STEP 12: Set image properties

Click on one of the **ImageSprites** to select it.

Picture

None
earL.png
earR.png
nose.png

Upload file...

Cancel   OK

Set its **Picture** property to be the nose.

Height

90 pixels...

Width

90 pixels...

Set its width and height to be around 90 pixels each.

Click another **ImageSprite**.

Set it to show one of the ears. Fix the height to be around 130 pixels, and the width to be about 65 pixels. Do the same for the other ear.

Height

130 pixels...

Width

65 pixels...

Picture

earL.png

Your design screen should look something like this.

STEP 13: Start coding

| Designer | Blocks |

Now switch to the **Blocks** view.

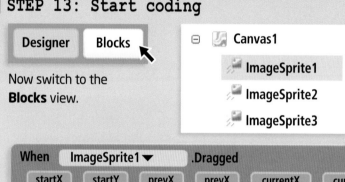

Start by clicking on the **ImageSprite1** icon in the blocks panel (on the left of the screen). See page 19 for help finding the other blocks. Drag them in to code your filter app.

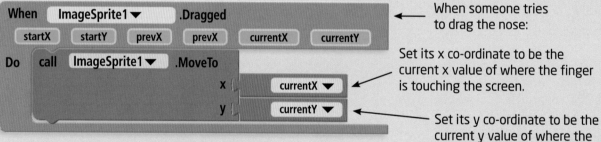

When someone tries to drag the nose:

Set its x co-ordinate to be the current x value of where the finger is touching the screen.

Set its y co-ordinate to be the current y value of where the finger is touching the screen.

Add similar code to make the ears draggable too.

Make sure these match.

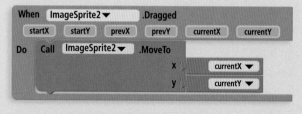

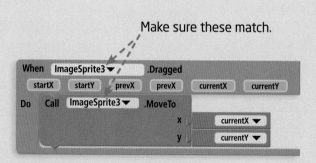

STEP 14: Code the camera

Add this code to make the camera work and save the final picture.

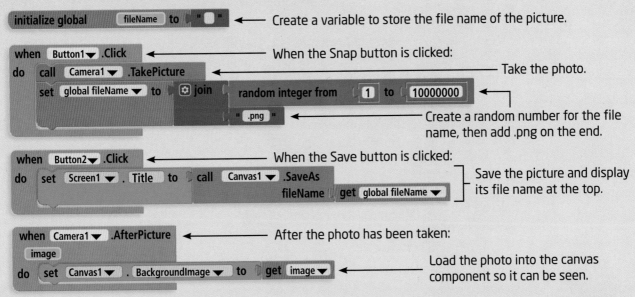

`initialize global` `fileName` `to` `" "` ← Create a variable to store the file name of the picture.

`when` `Button1 ▾` `.Click` ← When the Snap button is clicked:

`do` `call` `Camera1 ▾` `.TakePicture` ← Take the photo.

`set` `global fileName ▾` `to` `⚙ join` `random integer from` `1` `to` `10000000`

`" .png "` ← Create a random number for the file name, then add .png on the end.

`when` `Button2 ▾` `.Click` ← When the Save button is clicked:

`do` `set` `Screen1 ▾` `.` `Title` `to` `call` `Canvas1 ▾` `.SaveAs` `fileName` `get` `global fileName ▾`

Save the picture and display its file name at the top.

`when` `Camera1 ▾` `.AfterPicture` ← After the photo has been taken:

`image`

`do` `set` `Canvas1 ▾` `.` `BackgroundImage ▾` `to` `get` `image ▾`

Load the photo into the canvas component so it can be seen.

STEP 15: Test the app

`Connect ▾`
`AI Companion`
`Emulator`

Click the **Connect** menu, then choose the **AI Companion**. (Remember this won't work on the emulator.)

If you are using an Android device start the MIT AI Companion App, and connect it with the QR code option (see pages 14-15 for help).

The App should start. Take a photo, then drag the ears and mouth into position. Click Save when you are happy.

■ EXPERIMENT

Try changing the size of the filter features by altering their width and height properties.

Try downloading some different ears and noses - or other features, such as hats or glasses. Add the code to make them draggable (see box 13).

Make a completely new filter. Start by clicking **Projects - Save Project As** to duplicate your code. Download some new ears and other features. Upload these to your new project.

The Scratch Screen

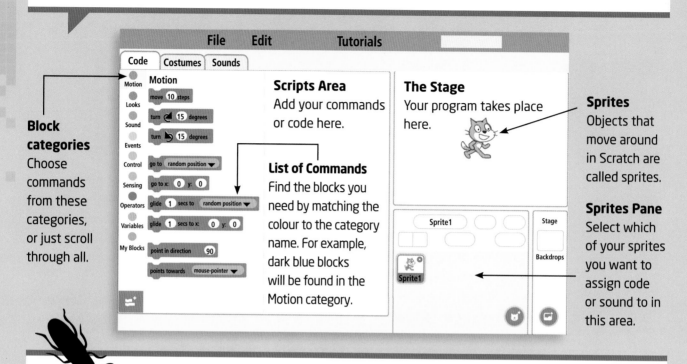

Block categories
Choose commands from these categories, or just scroll through all.

Scripts Area
Add your commands or code here.

List of Commands
Find the blocks you need by matching the colour to the category name. For example, dark blue blocks will be found in the Motion category.

The Stage
Your program takes place here.

Sprites
Objects that move around in Scratch are called sprites.

Sprites Pane
Select which of your sprites you want to assign code or sound to in this area.

Bugs & Debugging

When you find your code isn't working as expected, stop and look through each command you have put in. Think about what you want it to do and what it is really telling the computer to do. If you are entering one of the programs in this book, check your have not missed a line. Some things to check:

Scratch:

Select sprites before adding code:

Before you assign code to a sprite, click on it in the **Sprites pane**. This will select it and make sure the code is assigned to it.

Right colour, wrong code?

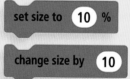

Be precise. Many code blocks look very similar but do completely different things!

App Inventor:

Can't connect?

If you can't connect App Inventor to your device or emulator try restarting them (see the bottom of page 14 and 15).

appinventor.mit.edu

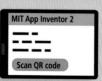

MIT App Inventor 2

Scan QR code

Not updating?

If you have changed some code but it's not running properly, try moving some of the components around. This will force App Inventor to run all the code again.

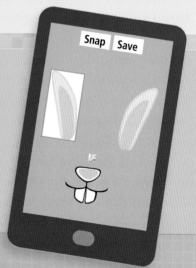

Tips to reduce bugs:

▶ When things are working properly spend time looking through your code so you understand each line. Experiment and change your code; try out different values. To be good at debugging, you need to understand what each part of your code does and how your code works.

▶ Practise debugging. Make a very short program and get a friend to change just one part of it while you aren't looking. Can you fix it?

▶ If you are making your own program, spend time drawing a diagram and planning it before you start. Try changing values if things don't work and don't be afraid to start again – you will learn from it.

Glossary

Bug
An error in a program that stops it working properly

Code block
A draggable instruction icon used in Scratch

Component
An object ,such as a button or label added to an app

Data
Information in an electronic form that can be stored and used by a computer

Debug
Removing bugs (or errors) from a program

Degrees
The units used to measure angles

Emulator
A 'virtual' smartphone or tablet running on a computer, behaving in the same way that a real device would

Event
Something that has happened while a program is running, such as a component being clicked or touched

Fax
a device or system used to send and receive documents in electronic form along a phone line

Greenwich meridian
the imaginary line from the North Pole to the South Pole that passes through Greenwich in England and marks 0° longitude, from which all other longitudes are measured

Hardware
The wires, chips, sensors and physical parts of a system or computer

Icon
A small clickable image on a computer, smartphone or tablet

Loop
Repeating one or more commands a number of times

Microprocessor
A part of a computer that controls its main operations

Pixel
A tiny dot on a screen, combined in their thousands to display pictures

Random
A number that can't be predicted

Right-click
Clicking the right mouse button on a sprite or icon

Sensor
A device that measures something in the real world, such as temperature, and sends it to a computer as a value

Software
A computer program containing instructions written in code

Sprite
An object with a picture on it that moves around the stage

Stage
The place in Scratch that sprites move around on

Steps
Small movements made by sprites

Variable
A value used to store information in a program that can change

Index

Further information

Generation Code: I'm an App Developer
by Max Wainewright (Wayland, 2018)

*Generation Code:
I'm an Advanced Scratch Coder*
by Max Wainewright (Wayland, 2018)

*Get Ahead in Computing:
Amazing Applications & Perfect Programs*
by Clive Gifford (Wayland, 2016)

Project Code series
by Kevin Wood (Frankin Watts, 2017)